Our Wedding

Our Wedding

A Book of Memories

by Eileen Kurtis-Kleinman

Designed and Illustrated by Judy Pelikan

A Welcome Book

Random House New York

ISBN 0-394-54515-X

Manufactured in the United States of America

9 8 7 6 5 4 3 2

FIRST EDITION

This book is
dedicated to us.
In it are preserved
some of the precious
beginning moments
that paved the road
on which we now travel
together.

With love for _____

From _____

Date _____

POPPY
•
D r e a m -
i -
n e s s
•

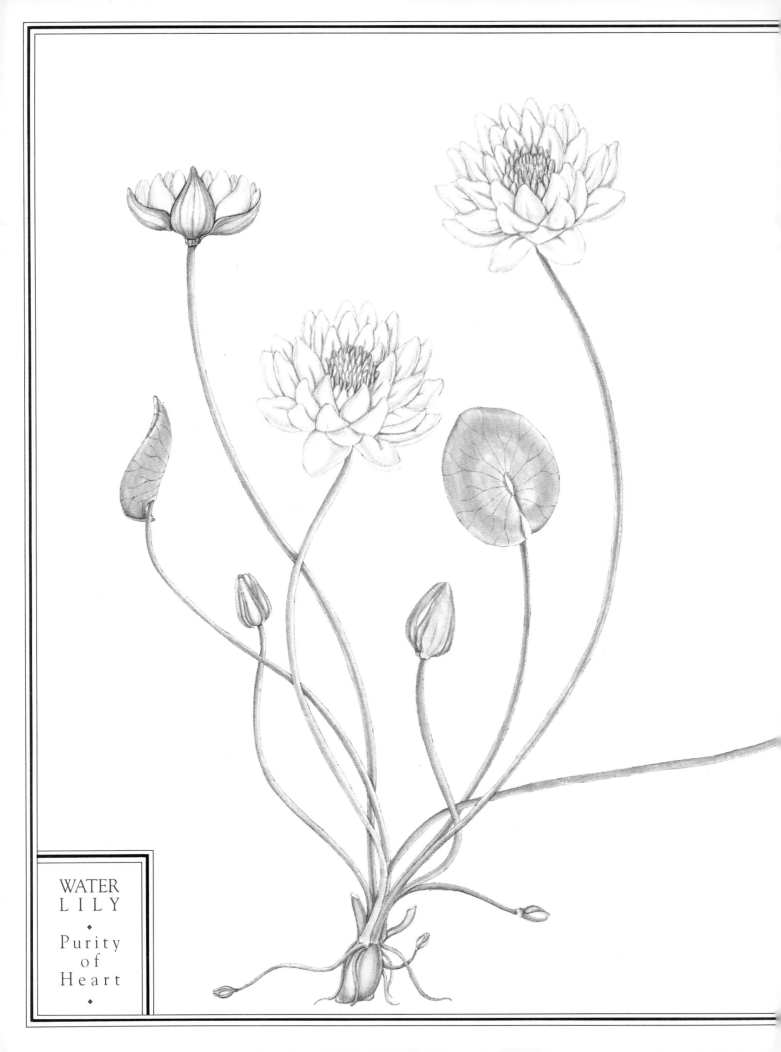

WATER
LILY
◆
Purity
of
Heart
◆

Contents

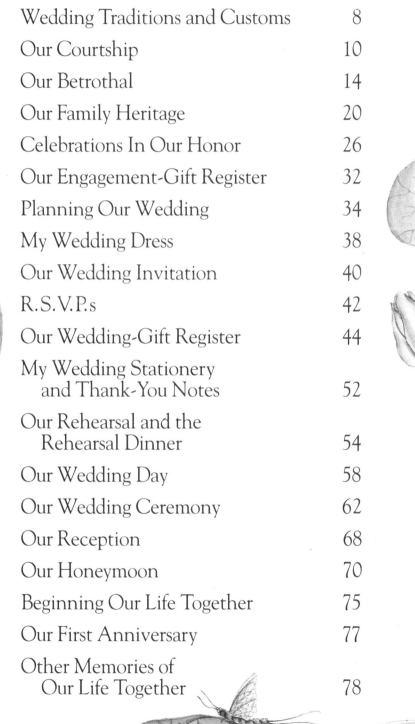

Wedding Traditions and Customs

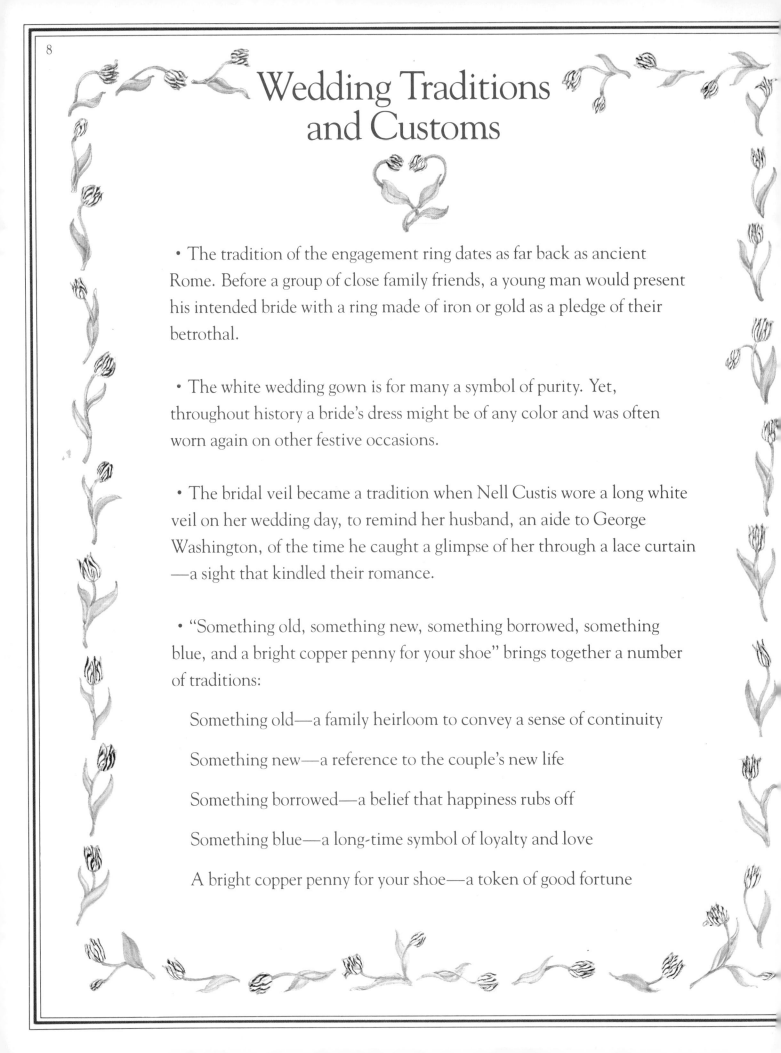

• The tradition of the engagement ring dates as far back as ancient Rome. Before a group of close family friends, a young man would present his intended bride with a ring made of iron or gold as a pledge of their betrothal.

• The white wedding gown is for many a symbol of purity. Yet, throughout history a bride's dress might be of any color and was often worn again on other festive occasions.

• The bridal veil became a tradition when Nell Custis wore a long white veil on her wedding day, to remind her husband, an aide to George Washington, of the time he caught a glimpse of her through a lace curtain —a sight that kindled their romance.

• "Something old, something new, something borrowed, something blue, and a bright copper penny for your shoe" brings together a number of traditions:

Something old—a family heirloom to convey a sense of continuity

Something new—a reference to the couple's new life

Something borrowed—a belief that happiness rubs off

Something blue—a long-time symbol of loyalty and love

A bright copper penny for your shoe—a token of good fortune

• A "ring cake," with the couple's initials on top and silver and gold charms baked inside, is often served at the rehearsal dinner. Women's charms are hidden under the bride's initials and the men's under the groom's. The cake is cut and distributed.

A woman who receives:

a ring—is the next to marry

a cat—will never marry

a heart—can look forward to romance

a thimble—will be very industrious

a coin—has fortune on her side

A man who receives:

a ring—is the next to marry

a dog or button—will remain a bachelor

a pair of dice—will have good luck

a coin—will have fortune smile on him

• The multi-tiered wedding cake grew out of an early Medieval English tradition that required the bridal couple to kiss over a stack of cakes, thus bringing good luck. In the seventeenth century an ingenious French baker joined the cakes with white icing.

• The ring, a symbol of eternity and age-old pledge of marriage, was supposedly first worn on the third finger by the early Egyptians, who believed that a special vein ran from that finger to the heart.

• Throwing rice—an ancient food staple—at the departing couple heralds a fertile marriage.

Our Courtship

Our
First
Meeting

I will always remember the first time I saw _____

_____

_____

When we first met, I remember feeling _____

_____

_____

I will never forget our first conversation… _____

_____

_____

Later he confided that he thought _____

_____

_____

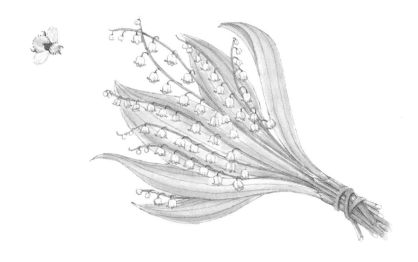

Photograph of us
during courtship

What I remember most about our first date _____

_____

_____

_____

I began to feel very special _____

_____

_____

The first time we kissed _____

_____

_____

I first realized I was in love _____

_____

_____

Even to this day, I begin to laugh when I remember _____

_____

_____

_____

Our Betrothal

CROCUS
·
Youth-
ful
Gladness
·

The story of our betrothal…

_____

_____

_____

_____

_____

_____

_____

_____

_____

_____

_____

_____

ANEMONE

•

E x -
pecta -
t i o n

•

The first person I shared the news of our engagement with was _____

_____

To celebrate, my future husband and I _____

_____

When I told my parents, they _____

_____

_____

_____

_____

For me, being engaged meant _____

_____

_____

_____

_____

When we first became engaged, these were some of our dreams for our life
together: _____

_____

_____

_____

_____

Engagement
Announcements

Engagement
Photographs
or Mementos

Our Family Heritage

Bride

_____

_____ _____

Brothers Sisters

_____ _____

Mother Father

_____ _____

Grandparents

_____ _____

_____ _____

Great-Grandparents

DAFFODIL
·
Regard
Chiv -
alry
·

Groom

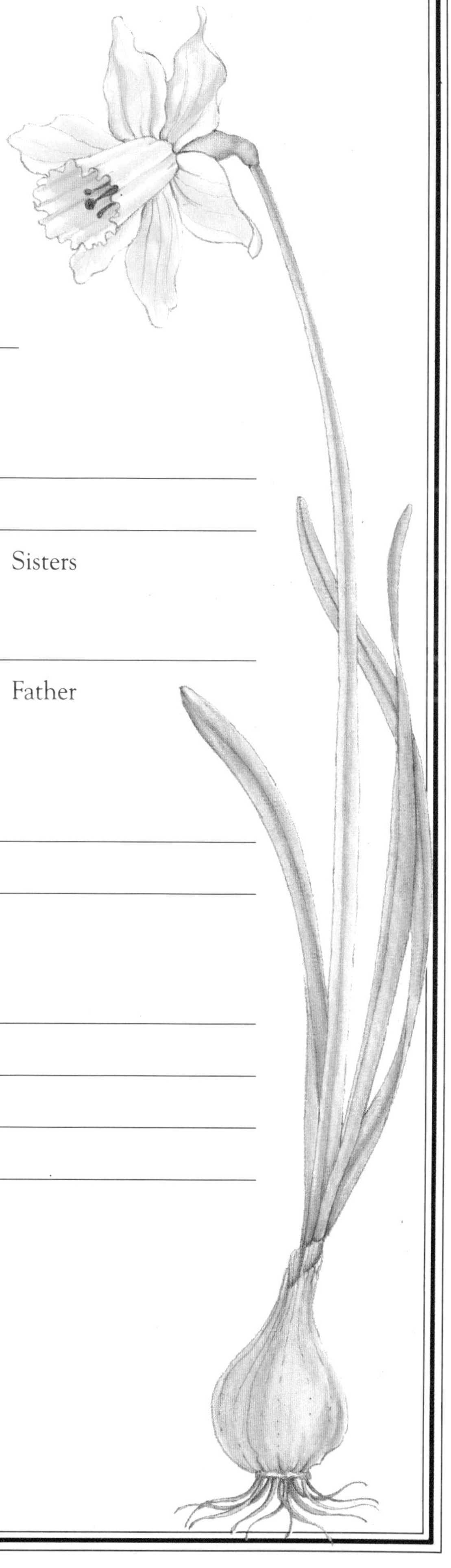

_____

_____

_____

Brothers

Sisters

_____

_____

Mother

Father

_____

_____

_____

_____

Grandparents

_____

_____

_____

_____

_____

_____

_____

_____

Great-Grandparents

My Husband's Family

Mother

His great-grandparents were born in

_____

on _____

His grandfather was born in

_____

on _____

His grandmother was born in

_____

on _____

His mother was born in

_____

on _____

Father

His great-grandparents were born in

_____

on _____

His grandfather was born in

_____

on _____

His grandmother was born in

_____

on _____

His father was born in

_____

on _____

Special people in the family tree: _____

_____

_____

My Family

Mother

My great-grandparents were born in

_____

on _____

My grandfather was born in

_____

on _____

My grandmother was born in

_____

on _____

My mother was born in

_____

on _____

Father

My great-grandparents were born in

_____

on _____

My grandfather was born in

_____

on _____

My grandmother was born in

_____

on _____

My father was born in

_____

on _____

Special people in the family tree: _____

_____

_____

Photograph of our
families

The day our families met each other we were glad that _____

_____

_____

I felt particularly welcomed by my new family when _____

_____

_____

_____

Photograph
of my husband
as a baby

Photograph
of me
as a baby

Celebrations
In Our Honor

Invitations

CLEMATIS
•
M e n t a l
B e a u t y
•

Mementos

Some of the special thoughts shared with us during the celebrations that I never want to forget were _____

_____

_____

_____

Some of the funniest moments I remember: _____

_____

_____

_____

I cried when _____

_____

Celebrating our betrothal made me feel _____

_____

_____

We were very surprised _____

_____

_____

My husband will always remember _____

_____

_____

Memorable Menus

Photographs

Photographs

Our Engagement-Gift Register

No.	Description

Given by   Purchased at   Acknowledged

Planning Our Wedding

When we began to think about our wedding, these were some of our dreams: _____

_____

_____

_____

_____

In planning our wedding, my husband and I felt most strongly about _____

_____

_____

_____

_____

Family traditions that my husband and I wanted to include: _____

_____

_____

_____

_____

_____

_____

_____

_____

PINKS
◆
Always
Lovely
Talent
◆

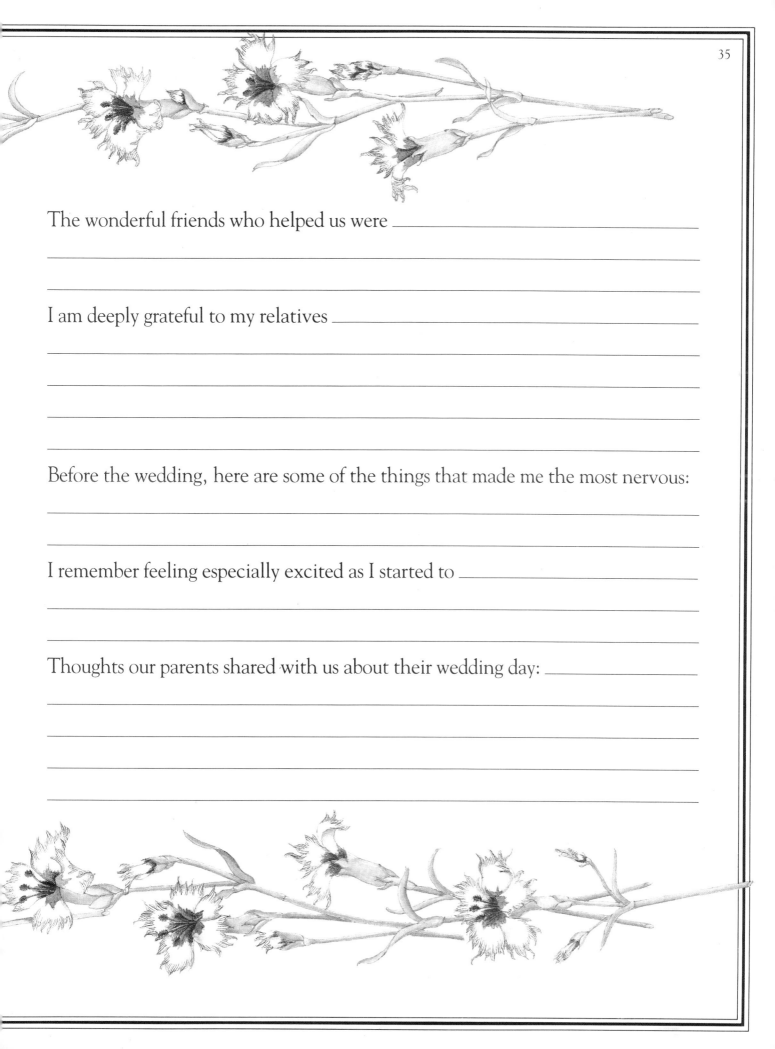

The wonderful friends who helped us were _____

_____

_____

I am deeply grateful to my relatives _____

_____

_____

_____

Before the wedding, here are some of the things that made me the most nervous:

_____

_____

I remember feeling especially excited as I started to _____

_____

_____

Thoughts our parents shared with us about their wedding day: _____

_____

_____

_____

We chose to be married at _____

because _____

_____

_____

We chose to be married by _____

because _____

_____

_____

Some of the special passages and prayers we included were _____

_____

_____

_____

_____

_____

_____

_____

_____

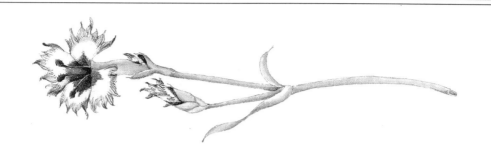

The music performed at our ceremony was _____

_____

_____

_____

For us this music had special meaning because _____

_____

_____

_____

The colors we chose as our wedding colors were _____

_____

because _____

_____

The flowers we chose had special meaning because _____

_____

_____

_____

My Wedding Dress

WHITE
ROSE

◆

I Am
Worthy
of You.

◆

When I went shopping for my dress, I'll always remember _____

_____

_____

When I first tried on my wedding dress, I felt _____

_____

_____

_____

I bought my dress at _____

_____

_____

With me at the time was _____

_____

_____

For my wedding day, my family saved a special keepsake for me, which was_____

_____

_____

_____

Our Wedding Invitation

ROSEBUD
•
P u r e
&
L o v e l y
•

Our Wedding
Invitation

R.S.V.P.s

Some of my favorite responses

PANSY
•
Thoughts
•

Our Wedding-Gift Register

IRIS
•
Promise
Faith
Elo-
quence
•

I registered our dinnerware patterns with _____

_____

Our china pattern is _____

_____

Our crystal pattern is _____

_____

Our silver pattern is _____

_____

Our Wedding-Gift Register

No.   Description

Given by   Purchased at   Acknowledged

No.   Description

Given by   Purchased at   Acknowledged

No.   Description

Given by   Purchased at   Acknowledged

My Wedding Stationery and Thank-You Notes

My
Wedding
Stationery

My
Thank-You
Notes

Our Rehearsal

One of the funniest things I remember about our rehearsal was _____

_____

_____

_____

The mistakes we made _____

_____

_____

_____

I was nervous about _____

_____

_____

_____

_____

_____

RED-
WHITE
ROSES
•
Unity
•

Our Rehearsal Dinner

The menu _____

_____

_____

_____

A special part of the dinner was when _____

_____

_____

_____

_____

The cleverest toast _____

_____

_____

The toast that brought tears to my eyes _____

_____

_____

_____

Photograph

Our Wedding Attendants

Bride's

My Maid of Honor _____

My Bridesmaids _____

_____

_____

_____

_____

Flower Children _____

_____

_____

_____

Groom's

Best Man _____

Groomsmen _____

_____

_____

_____

_____

_____

Our Wedding Day

Date

Photograph
of Bride

I will always remember the feeling that I had on the morning of our wedding day

_____

_____

_____

My wish for that day was _____

_____

_____

Standing in front of the mirror in my bridal dress, I remember feeling _____

_____

_____

_____

I will never forget the moment he first saw me as his bride _____

_____

_____

_____

_____

_____

Our Wedding Ceremony

MOSS
ROSE
•
Confes-
s i o n
of Love
•

These were the vows we exchanged: _____

_____

_____

_____

_____

_____

_____

Standing next to my husband as we were being married, I remember thinking ____

_____

_____

_____

I felt especially beautiful when _____

_____

_____

I felt like crying when _____

_____

_____

_____

Ceremony
Memento

Ceremony
Memento

Photograph
of our
wedding ceremony

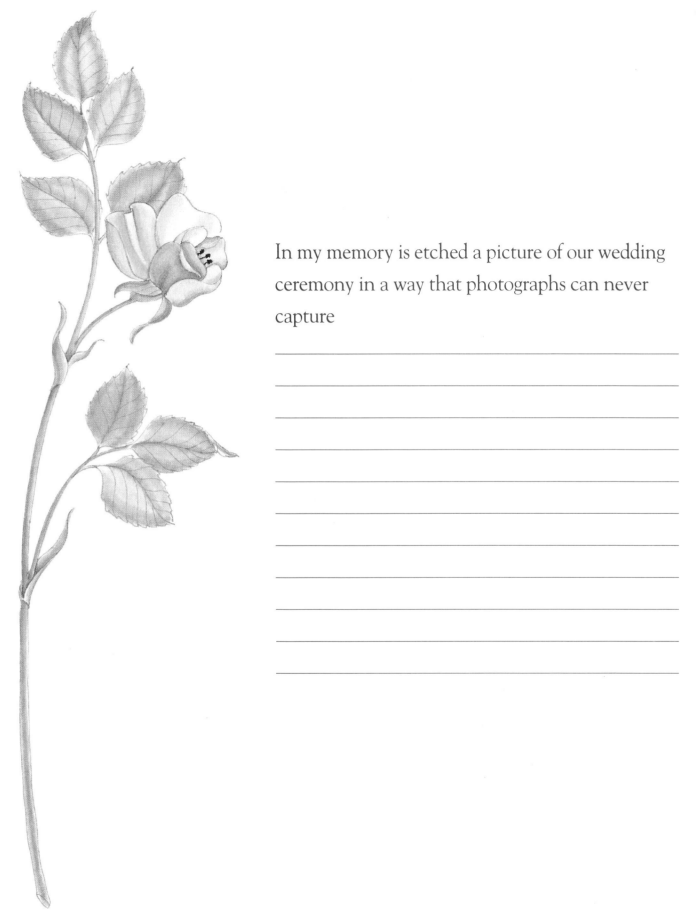

In my memory is etched a picture of our wedding ceremony in a way that photographs can never capture

Our Reception

Memento

Photograph

ORANGE
BLOSSOM
◆
B r i d a l
F e s t i v -
i t i e s
◆

Our reception was held _____

_____

_____

We arrived at the reception _____

_____

_____

The music for our celebration _____

_____

When I first danced with my husband _____

_____

_____

Some wonderful toasts I will always remember ___

_____

_____

_____

I particularly felt love for my husband when ____

_____

_____

_____

Our Honeymoon

MORNING
GLORY
•
Depart-
ure
Fare-
well

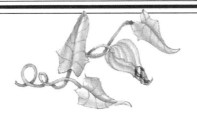

For our honeymoon we _____

_____

_____

_____

Special places we visited _____

_____

Some of our most romantic moments _____

_____

_____

_____

Some of the funniest moments _____

_____

_____

_____

Memorable meals _____

_____

_____

_____

_____

Photographs
of our
honeymoon

Photographs
of our
honeymoon

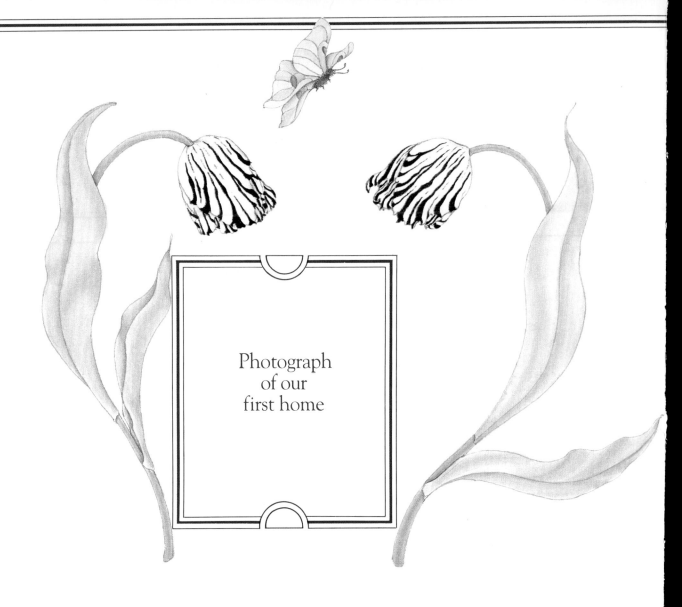

Photograph
of our
first home

Our address was _____

_____

I will always remember our first home because _____

_____

_____

_____

TULIPS
•
Declar-
a t i o n
o f
L o v e
•

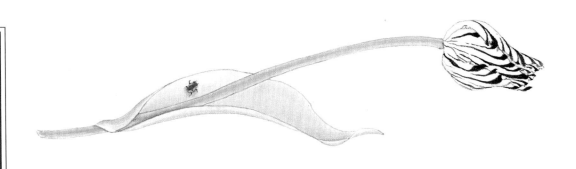

Beginning Our Life Together

When we were first married, we loved to _____
_____
_____
_____

Some of my husband's quirks and foibles I learned to indulge: _____
_____
_____
_____

As a newlywed, my husband couldn't understand my habit of _____
_____
_____
_____

The interests we have cultivated together: _____
_____
_____
_____
_____

Photograph
or Memento
of our
first anniversary

Our First Anniversary

For our first anniversary we _____

_____

_____

_____

I gave him _____

_____

He gave me _____

_____

The discoveries we made in ourselves _____

_____

_____

_____

Being married has new meaning to us now. _____

_____

_____

_____

Advice we would give about getting married: _____

_____

_____

_____

Other Memories
of Our Life Together